What if we do
NOTHING?

AIDS
AND OTHER EPIDEMICS

Carol Ballard

FRANKLIN WATTS
LONDON • SYDNEY

First published in 2009 by Franklin Watts

Copyright © 2009 Arcturus Publishing Limited

Franklin Watts
338 Euston Road
London NW1 3BH

Franklin Watts Australia
Level 17/207 Kent Street, Sydney, NSW 2000

Produced by Arcturus Publishing Limited,
26/27 Bickels Yard, 151-153 Bermondsey Street,
London SE1 3HA

Series concept: Alex Woolf
Editor: Alex Woolf
Designer: Phipps Design
Picture researcher: Alex Woolf

The illustrations and diagrams on pages 15, 16,
19, 20, 27, 35 and 39 are by Phipps Design.

A CIP catalogue record for this book is available
from the British Library.

Dewey Decimal Classification Number: 614.4

ISBN 978 0 7496 8745 8

Printed in China

Franklin Watts is a division of Hachette
Children's Books, an Hachette Livre UK company.
www.hachettelivre.co.uk

Picture Credits
Corbis: cover bottom left (Gideon Mendel), cover top right (Erik de
Castro), 5 (Jose L Pelaez), 7 (Stefano Bianchetti), 12 (Gideon
Mendel), 14 (Bettmann), 18 (Karen Kasmauski), 23 (Reuters),
24 (Reuters), 26 (Visuals Unlimited), 34 (CDC/PHIL), 36 (Louise
Gubb), 43 (CDC/PHIL), 45 (Karen Kasmauski).
Getty Images: 11 (MPI/Stringer), 17 (Robert Giroux), 40 (Andrew
Caballero-Reynolds).
Science Photo Library: cover background (Mehau Kulyk), 9
(NIBSC), 28 (AJ Photo/Hop Americain), 30 (London School of
Hygiene and Tropical Medicine), 32 (Philippepsaila), 39 (Paul
Whitehill).

Cover pictures
bottom left: A young South African woman with HIV.
top right: People in Manila, Philippines, light candles to mark World
AIDS Day.
background: An illustration of HIV particles.

Contents

CHAPTER 1

Epidemic!

It is 2025. Emergency workers are practising their response to a major breakout of an infectious disease. Health workers, police and even the army, navy and air force are involved. Health workers are distributing vaccines to protect key workers. They are also practising diagnosing cases of the disease and deciding who needs to go to hospital and who should be sent home. The police and army are responsible for enforcing quarantine areas to prevent the disease spreading. The army and navy are patrolling borders, ports and airports to prevent more cases arriving from other countries. Luckily, it is all just a practice. It is only a matter of time, however, before it will be for real.

What are infectious diseases?

Infectious diseases are illnesses that can pass from one person to another, such as chickenpox, influenza and meningitis. Under normal conditions, only a few people in a population tend to suffer from a particular infectious disease. A localized outbreak occurs when the number of cases of the disease increases rapidly within a small area. If the disease spreads more widely, affecting people over a larger area or even a whole country, the outbreak is called an epidemic. If an outbreak spreads over an even larger area, covering several countries, a continent or – in the worst cases – the whole world, it is called a pandemic.

What causes infectious diseases and how do they spread?

Infectious diseases are caused by micro-organisms, or germs. These tiny life-forms are too small to see with the naked eye. They include bacteria, viruses, fungi and parasites. There are several ways in which

DETECTING AND MONITORING EPIDEMICS

The sooner an outbreak of an infectious disease is detected, the sooner action can be taken to minimize its spread. Orbiting satellites from the National Aeronautics and Space Administration (NASA) collect global environmental data daily. This is passed on to scientists who use it to help them predict and track outbreaks of disease. This information gives governments and health organizations more time to respond to an outbreak and take appropriate action.

infectious diseases can spread from one person to another.

- **By air** When you cough or sneeze, air and droplets of liquid are expelled from your body very quickly. Germs spread into the air around you, and can then be breathed in by anybody who is close.
- **By water** Some germs thrive in dirty water. They enter the body when someone drinks the dirty water, or uses it for cooking.
- **By food** Good storage keeps food free from disease-causing micro-organisms. Cooking food kills any micro-organisms that happen to be present in it. Poor food hygiene and inadequate cooking can allow micro-organisms to multiply in the food and infect anyone who eats it.
- **By direct contact** Some infectious diseases are spread by direct contact with someone who is already infected. This might be by touch, or by mixing of body fluids such as saliva and blood.
- **By insects and other animals** Insects and other animals can also spread infections. For example, some disease-causing micro-organisms are spread when an infected insect bites a person. A living thing that transmits an infection between individuals of another species is called a vector.

This boy has a cold. By using his handkerchief when he sneezes, he can reduce the chances of passing the infection on to other people.

Fighting infections

Your body has a natural defence mechanism. It is called your immune system. When your body encounters a disease-causing micro-organism such as a virus or bacterium for the first time, your immune system makes chemicals called antibodies to help fight the infection. The process of fighting the infection takes a little time, during which you will probably be ill. The next time the same micro-organism enters your body, however, your immune system is prepared. It recognizes the micro-organism and responds swiftly so that you do not become ill. You are said to be immune to the infection.

Why do epidemics occur?

Most people will have experienced a localized outbreak of a particular infection, such as an upset stomach. An outbreak begins with a few cases. In a short time, a large number of people within a small area are infected. Then the outbreak slowly dies away. An epidemic arises when the number of cases does not die away but increases, and the area covered grows larger.

Epidemics can arise for a variety of reasons. Within any population, a proportion of people will be immune to an infectious disease. The infection does not affect everybody. However, many viruses and bacteria can change, or mutate, giving rise to new types. When this happens, even fewer people will be immune to the new type. The infection will affect a large number of people and spread rapidly over a wider area – an epidemic occurs.

Another way an epidemic can occur is if an infectious disease that is common in one part of the world is taken to another part of the world. The people there will not have been exposed to that infection before and so nobody will be immune to it. This has happened in the past, with infections being carried by traders, armies and explorers as they moved from country to country. When Europeans came to the Americas, they brought smallpox, a highly contagious disease, to the continent. Scientists estimate that smallpox may have killed 20 million people, or 95 per cent of the native population.

VACCINES AND VACCINATION

Vaccination is a way of generating immunity to an infection. To do this, a substance called a vaccine is given to the patient, either by mouth or injection. The vaccine contains dead or weakened viruses and bacteria. These cannot cause an infection, but they stimulate the immune system in the same way as the live micro-organisms would. This means that if the person encounters the live micro-organisms in the future, the immune system responds quickly, preventing the person from becoming infected.

Environmental effects

Infectious diseases, especially those that are spread by dirty water, can reach epidemic proportions in places where large numbers of people live in cramped conditions with poor sanitation. This is the situation in some developing countries, and in places like refugee camps.

Modern travel

In the modern world, global air travel helps germs spread quickly and widely. Epidemics can occur very rapidly, becoming pandemics as they spread across large areas of the world.

Many people died during a cholera epidemic in Paris in 1832. The squalid living conditions shown in the picture were probably partly to blame.

DEBATE

You are in charge

As a medical advisor to the government you have been asked to come up with a way to detect epidemics early. To do that, you need information. Which of the following, do you think, would be most helpful?

■ Ask doctors to report the number of cases of infectious diseases that they diagnose each week.

■ Keep a map showing the location of every reported case and how that changes with time.

■ Create a database containing the details of each person infected, including their age, sex, ethnic group and recent journeys made.

CHAPTER 2

HIV/AIDS

It is 2025. The HIV/AIDS crisis has reached a critical level in many countries. People all around the world are infected. Millions of people have died from the disease and many more are very ill. Large numbers of children are orphaned and resources are stretched as governments and aid agencies struggle to look after them all properly. Governments and health groups are organizing campaigns to tell people about HIV/AIDS and the steps each individual can take to guard against infection. Scientists are searching desperately to find a cure for HIV/AIDS. Others are trying to develop a vaccine to protect people against infection. Medicines are available to treat the illness but they are so expensive that many people cannot afford them.

What causes HIV/AIDS?

AIDS stands for Acquired Immune Deficiency Syndrome. When the first cases were reported in the United States in 1981, nobody knew what caused it. In 1983, scientists in France and the United States identified a virus they called Human Immunodeficiency Virus (HIV) as the cause of AIDS. Two years later, blood tests to detect the presence of HIV in patients were developed. People who are infected with HIV are said to be HIV positive (HIV+).

Where did HIV/AIDS come from?

Many infectious diseases have been known about for hundreds of years. HIV/AIDS, however, appeared to be a completely new disease. Most scientists believe HIV/AIDS arose in Sub-Saharan Africa. Many think it likely that it first appeared in monkeys and then crossed over into humans. From there, it spread rapidly throughout Sub-Saharan Africa and to the rest of the world.

Effects of HIV/AIDS

The body's immune system protects people from infections and other diseases. HIV attacks and destroys the immune system, so the person's defences against other infections and diseases are weakened. Therefore, people with HIV become ill with many diseases that a healthy immune system would be able to ward off. People can remain HIV+ for many years. Eventually, however, the illness progresses to its final stages, which is called AIDS. The person becomes increasingly ill from infections and other complications such as cancers, which ultimately cause death.

Diagnosing HIV/AIDS

Infection with HIV can be diagnosed by testing for antibodies in a sample of blood, urine or saliva. However, as there can be a time delay of several months between infection and the appearance of the antibodies, this is not always ideal. A more immediate diagnosis can be made by testing for chemicals of HIV particles.

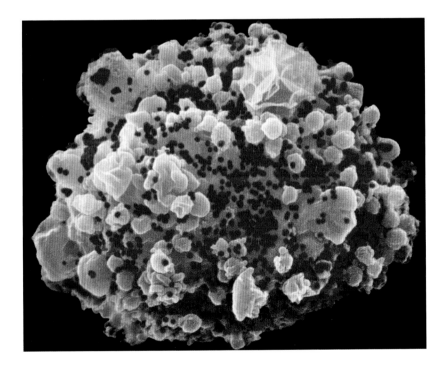

The white blood cell in this micrograph (a photo of an image seen through a microscope) is infected with HIV, seen here as red dots. The virus kills the white blood cells, weakening the immune system.

What are the symptoms of HIV/AIDS?

People who are infected with HIV suffer from repeated infections, especially colds, coughs and chest infections. In later stages, diarrhoea becomes common. Fevers, chills, weakness and weight loss, together with infections and tumours, are characteristic of the final stages of AIDS.

How does HIV/AIDS spread?

HIV/AIDS cannot spread simply by day-to-day contact with an HIV+ person. You can't get it by hugging a person. It's not spread through the air, like a cold. For a healthy person to become infected with HIV, their body fluids must mix with body fluids from an HIV+ person. There are several ways this can happen:

- **Sexual contact** In most cases of HIV infection, the infection is spread by sexual contact. That can be avoided by sexual abstinence, faithfulness in a lasting relationship or by practising safe sex.
- **Exposure to HIV+ blood** In the early days of AIDS, people who received blood transfusions often became infected with HIV. Then scientists learned more about AIDS and HIV, and how it is spread. Today, in developed countries, HIV infection from blood and blood products is rare, as blood is routinely screened before use to make sure it is not HIV+. In many developing countries, however, blood is not screened for HIV and therefore infections still occur in this way.
- **Mother-to-child contact** HIV can pass from mother to child during the last weeks of pregnancy, or during a normal birth. The risk can be greatly reduced if the mother is given drug treatment during pregnancy, and if the baby is born by caesarean section.
- **Other routes** Health workers exposed to HIV-infected blood take many safety precautions. However, they are still at risk if the virus enters their body. An infected needle, for instance, might accidentally pierce their skin through the rubber gloves they wear. Without proper safety precautions, tattooing and body piercing also pose a risk if needles become contaminated with infected blood. Drug addicts who share needles are at high risk from HIV infection.

Who does HIV/AIDS affect?

HIV/AIDS affects a wide variety of people. It cuts across race, age, gender, social and geographical boundaries. In the United States, the first cases reported were in homosexual men. However, the disease is widespread among heterosexuals, infecting men and women in equal numbers globally.

RYAN WHITE

In 1984, a boy named Ryan White contracted HIV/AIDS after receiving a transfusion of HIV-infected blood. At the time, little was known about HIV/AIDS and how it spread. Many people were afraid of getting the disease. Ryan, then 13, was banned from his school. He and his family were shunned by the community in his hometown of Kokomo, Indiana, USA. People were so hostile that his family eventually decided to move to Cicero, Indiana. Ryan's experience with HIV/AIDS and the way he and his family had been treated drew national media attention. Ryan spoke up for people with HIV/AIDS and campaigned for people to treat them fairly and with dignity. Ryan died in 1990 at the age of 18. Later that year, Congress passed the Ryan White Comprehensive AIDS Resources Emergency (CARE) Act, which ensures financial support for people living with HIV/AIDS. Sadly, many people still do not know all the facts about HIV/AIDS. In many places, people with the disease and their families are still treated like outcasts.

Each year, the number of people infected with HIV increases. In 2007, UNAIDS and the World Health Organization reported that, globally, 33.2 million people were living with HIV. That figure included 2.5 million children under the age of 15. That year, about 2.5 million people were newly infected with the virus and 2.1 million people died of AIDS.

Sub-Saharan Africa has been hardest hit by the epidemic. Nearly two-thirds of all HIV-infected people live in that region. About 61 per cent of all adults infected there are women. If we do nothing, some people think that by 2025, the death toll from AIDS in Africa alone since 1980 could add up to 60 million adults and 15 million children. As many as 22.4 million African children could be orphaned.

After Ryan White was diagnosed with HIV/AIDS, he had to fight a long legal battle to be allowed to continue his education. His campaign turned him into a national celebrity and spokesman for AIDS awareness.

Treating HIV/AIDS

Medicines are available to treat people diagnosed as being HIV+. However, these medicines only delay the progression of the illness – there is as yet no known cure.

A common approach to treating HIV/AIDS is known as HAART (highly active antiretroviral therapy). Patients take a mixture of several drugs to stabilize their symptoms and to reduce the amount of virus in their body. This can improve their general health and increase their survival time, but not all patients are able to maintain the HAART treatment. Some experience unpleasant side effects, while others find the process too complicated.

Antiretroviral drugs are very expensive and need to be taken for the rest of a person's life. Many HIV/AIDS patients can't afford the drugs, especially in developing countries where they are desperately needed.

New drugs

Researchers are trying to develop new, more effective drugs to treat HIV/AIDS. They have been assisted in this task by recent advances in the science of genetics. For example, some researchers are hoping to develop a drug that will switch off HIV, putting the virus into

Here, a health worker is explaining the HIV test to some children before she tests them. Their mother is HIV+ but luckily the tests showed none of the children was infected.

'hibernation'. The person would still be infected, but the virus would not multiply, so the person would not become ill.

Preventing infection

Education programmes have been introduced in some countries to tell people about HIV/AIDS and how they can avoid becoming infected. In some places, free condoms are available to reduce infection by sexual contact. In other places, needle exchange programmes can help drug addicts to avoid infection.

Search for a vaccine

Vaccination can provide a way of protecting the body from infection. Chemicals in the vaccine boost the immune system. Then, when a disease-causing micro-organism enters the body, the strengthened immune system responds rapidly and destroys it. As every micro-organism is different, a vaccine can only offer protection against a single micro-organism. Scientists are trying to develop a vaccine that will offer protection against HIV. Their work is hampered by the fact that, like most viruses, HIV does not stay the same. It changes, or mutates, over time. This means that the vaccine also has to be altered to match the new version of the virus.

DEBATE

You are in charge

You are a health official in a country with an increasing number of HIV/AIDS cases. You have limited funding. What percentage of your money do you spend on the following?

■ trying to reduce the number of new cases by educating the general public about how to avoid infection.

■ buying drugs to treat those already ill, to maintain their health for longer.

■ scientific research to develop a vaccine, to prevent new cases arising.

Which option or options would you choose to control the spread of HIV/AIDS, now and in the future?

CHAPTER 3

Influenza

It is 2025. The world is in the grip of a global influenza pandemic. International travel is restricted. Within individual countries, travel restrictions and quarantine zones are in force. Hospitals are overwhelmed and many people who really need hospital treatment have to stay at home. Drugs for treating the sick are running out. Factories and schools are closed. Theatres, cinemas, restaurants and other places where large numbers of people gather are also shut. Graves cannot be dug quickly enough to bury the dead. Food stocks are running short and other vital services such as water and electricity supplies are failing. People are scared and governments seem powerless to improve the situation.

Could influenza really be that bad?

Most people think of influenza – or flu, as it is usually called – as a sort of very bad cold. Influenza can be deadly, though, especially for young children and the elderly. In a normal year, ten to twenty per cent of the population of the United States will suffer from influenza, with about 36,000 dying from complications. In a major epidemic, the figures would be much, much higher.

Volunteers in Cincinnati, Ohio, USA, feed the children of families struck down by the 1918 influenza pandemic. Many people wore face masks to try to avoid becoming infected.

Influenza pandemic in 1918

In March 1918, during World War I, an influenza outbreak began in an army camp in Kansas, USA. Another outbreak began in Europe around the same time. No one knows for sure where the flu originated, but research suggests it may have come from Asia. Soldiers from both the USA and Europe carried the infection with them, helping it to spread rapidly. By August,

the epidemic was gaining strength, becoming a worldwide pandemic during the winter of 1918/19. Unlike most flu viruses, this one killed not just children and the elderly but also healthy people in their 20s and 30s. It is estimated that more than 20 per cent of the world's population became ill, and between 2.5 per cent and 5 per cent – more than 50 million people – died.

Learning from the past

If the same proportion of today's global population of 6.6 billion people were to be affected by an influenza pandemic, more than 1.3 billion people would become ill and between 165 and 300 million people would die. Luckily, though, we can learn lessons from the past. The World Health Organization (WHO) and other agencies monitor outbreaks of many different infections, including influenza. Governments have plans that can be put into action fast if an epidemic begins. Some supplies of vaccine are available to protect key workers such as medical staff and those involved in maintaining vital services. More doses of vaccine could be produced in a relatively short time for other people. Health experts hope that if another major epidemic broke out, these measures would enable authorities to contain it and reduce its impact.

This map shows the World Health Organization's surveillance network, which monitors the world for outbreaks of influenza epidemics. The countries in red have a national network of laboratories. The orange countries have more than one laboratory, and the yellow countries have just one WHO laboratory. The blue countries have no laboratories.

Source: www.brown.edu/Courses/Bio_160/Projects1999/flu/epidemiology.html

What causes influenza?

Influenza is caused by influenza viruses. There are many different influenza viruses but they fall into three categories, known as types A, B and C. Types A and B can cause human influenza epidemics. Type C usually only causes mild cases of flu. The outer coat of each influenza virus contains two proteins, known as H and N, each of which can exist in several different forms. Each form is given a number, such as H1 or H2. The combination of different H and N forms is used to identify the influenza strains. For example, the Spanish flu virus responsible for the 1918 pandemic was the H1N1 strain.

New strains

Like other viruses, an influenza virus can mutate over time, giving rise to new strains of the virus. The new strains will be similar to the original in some ways but different in other ways. An influenza epidemic is usually caused by a strain of virus that has not been seen before. This is because very few people in the population will be immune to the virus and therefore the infection rates will be very high. If the same strain appears a second time, many people will be immune from their previous exposure to it and so the outbreak will be much less serious.

TIMELINE OF INFLUENZA EPIDEMICS

This timeline shows some of the major influenza epidemics and pandemics that occurred during the 20th and early 21st centuries.

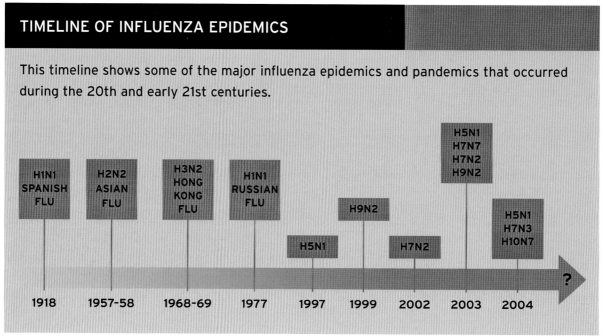

Source: www.news.cornell.edu/stories/Oct05/Avian_Torres.kr.html

What are the symptoms of influenza?

Influenza viruses cause a variety of symptoms. The most common symptoms are shivering and body aches, a headache, coughing and chest pains. A fever develops rapidly and lasts for several days. Afterwards, a patient often feels tired and weak, and sometimes rather depressed, for a week or more.

Most influenza infections are more serious in the elderly and in young children. Complications such as chest infections often follow a bout of influenza. These aren't caused by the flu virus but by other infections picked up while the body is weakened.

How is influenza treated?

Some antiviral drugs can be used to treat influenza, but in most cases the infection is allowed to run its course, relying on the patient's own immune system to overcome it. Most medicines sold as flu remedies are designed to make the patient feel better, but they do not actually cure the infection.

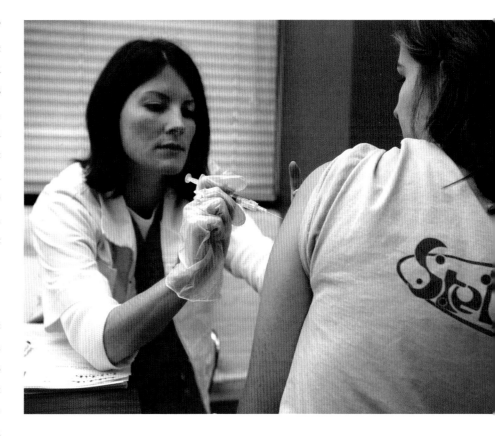

Vaccination

Vaccines provide some protection from influenza infection. In some countries these are made available every year to the elderly, to children and to people with medical conditions, such as asthma, for whom influenza would be most serious. However, vaccine makers can only predict which of the many strains of influenza will be the next to emerge. If an unexpected strain of the virus causes an outbreak, they have to rush to make a specific vaccine to fight it. The protection offered by an influenza vaccine is not long-lived, so many people have an annual vaccination each autumn.

Many people in the developed world are now regularly vaccinated against influenza, like this girl.

Avian influenza – 'bird flu'

In recent years, there have been numerous reports in the media about outbreaks of 'bird flu'. Some experts have predicted that a bird flu pandemic is very likely in the near future. So what is bird flu, and why are some people so worried about it?

Bird flu is the common name for an infection called avian influenza. It is a type of influenza that affects birds, hence its name. Wild birds carry the virus in their bodies, but it does not usually make them ill. However, they can pass it on via body fluids and waste to domesticated birds such as chickens, turkeys and ducks. The infection makes these birds very ill and, in many cases, it is fatal. Bird flu can spread rapidly through poultry flocks, with devastating effects.

Which viruses are involved?

The viruses responsible for bird flu are type A influenza viruses. There are different strains, each with a particular combination of H and N proteins in its coat, just like the viruses that cause human influenza.

A girl herds ducks through pig pens in a village in China. The chance of an influenza infection passing from species to species is increased in crowded conditions like these.

How can they affect humans?

Avian influenza viruses can infect humans, but usually only people who have been in very close contact with infected birds. Symptoms in humans include fever, cough, aches and breathing difficulties. It is very rare for avian influenza to be passed from one person to another.

Why are people worried about a bird flu pandemic?

One strain of avian influenza virus, called H5N1, is known to spread very quickly among birds and to have a high mortality rate. H5N1 does not usually infect people but when it does it is very dangerous and sometimes fatal, even in healthy people. It is a strain that mutates rapidly. People worry that the virus could mutate in humans in a way that makes it easier to spread from person to person.

When a virus infects a person or animal, it reproduces rapidly. If the person or animal is infected by two different viruses at the same time, the combination can create a new virus. This will have some characteristics of each of the original viruses.

The transition from an infection in wild birds to an infection that passes rapidly from person to person would have several stages (see diagram on the right). Scientists are worried that this sequence of events could result in a highly infectious and very dangerous virus. This could cause an epidemic or even a worldwide pandemic. Although H5N1 seems to be the virus strain that is most likely to be involved, other possible strains that are being monitored include H7N1 and H9N2.

This diagram illustrates how a new hybrid virus could arise from the mixing of an avian influenza virus and a human influenza virus.

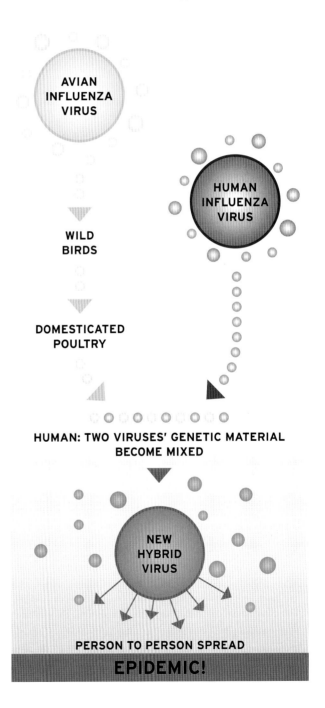

AVIAN INFLUENZA VIRUS

WILD BIRDS

DOMESTICATED POULTRY

HUMAN INFLUENZA VIRUS

HUMAN: TWO VIRUSES' GENETIC MATERIAL BECOME MIXED

NEW HYBRID VIRUS

PERSON TO PERSON SPREAD

EPIDEMIC!

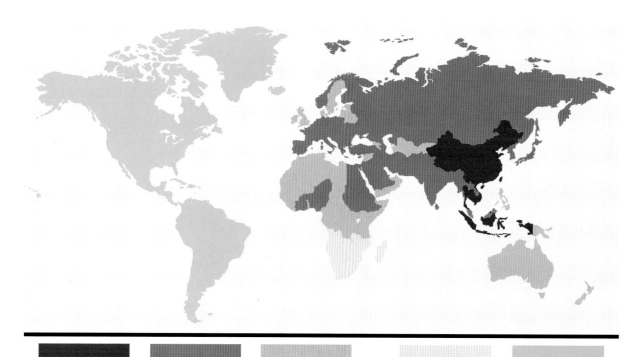

endemic Some cases already occurring all the time among people and animals

epidemic Some occasional outbreaks in animals

high risk Near to countries with human or animal cases, or at risk from bird migration and/or transport

at risk Bird migration and/or transport may lead to animal cases

pandemic risk Animal cases are unlikely, but would be affected by a human pandemic

Source: www.usaid.gov/our_work/global_health/home/News/news_items/avian_influenza.html

Human cases of bird flu

The World Health Organization tracks cases of bird flu in people. The number of H5N1 infections appears to be growing and spreading.

- **1997** Several hundred people became infected with the H5N1 virus in Hong Kong, and six people died. To prevent the spread of this virus, all the chickens in Hong Kong were killed.
- **2004** Forty-six infections of H5N1 were reported in Thailand and Vietnam, resulting in 32 deaths.
- **2005** Ninety-eight cases of H5N1 infections were confirmed in Vietnam, Thailand, China, Cambodia and Indonesia, resulting in 43 deaths.
- **2006** There were 115 cases of H5N1 infections confirmed in nine countries in Asia and the Middle East, resulting in 79 deaths.
- **2007** Nine countries, including two in Africa, reported a total of 88 cases of H5N1 flu, resulting in 59 deaths

This world map shows the risk posed to each country by avian influenza.

Minimizing the risk of a bird flu epidemic

Governments and international organizations are very aware of the potential risk of a bird flu epidemic or pandemic in humans. Several plans are in place to minimize this risk. They include the following:

- **Monitoring wild and domesticated birds worldwide** Wild birds are monitored, especially along migration routes. Any domesticated birds found to be infected are culled, along with the rest of the flock to which they belong. Farms, nature reserves and other premises can be quarantined. Farmers can be ordered to bring domesticated poultry indoors if the birds are at risk.
- **Global reporting and information exchange** This allows information to be accessed quickly and appropriate actions taken.
- **Vaccination** Birds close to an outbreak may be vaccinated in an attempt to prevent the spread of the infection.
- **Changing farming methods** Close contact between birds and people has been reduced where possible. However, many poorer rural communities find it hard to change their traditional lifestyle, with birds and people living closely together. A bird flu epidemic in humans is therefore more likely to arise in a traditional rural area.
- **Improving veterinary services** Having more qualified and experienced veterinary personnel increases the chance of containing an outbreak quickly and efficiently.

If an epidemic begins ...

There are plans in place in case an outbreak of bird flu begins to spread from person to person. These include stockpiling antiviral drugs for rapid distribution to people at risk. Some countries have the ability to produce large amounts of vaccine very quickly. Sharing information between countries could reduce the time it takes to identify the virus and develop a vaccine.

DEBATE

You are in charge
There is a major outbreak of avian influenza in humans, and vaccine supplies are limited. As the government official responsible for health, do you order medical staff to:

- vaccinate as many people as possible – first come, first served
- vaccinate anybody who can afford to pay
- vaccinate key workers only
- vaccinate the vulnerable only

Which approach do you think would be the most effective way to use your vaccine stocks and why?

CHAPTER 4

SARS

It is 2025. An outbreak of severe acute respiratory syndrome (SARS) has been confirmed. The number of people infected has increased rapidly to epidemic levels. The first cluster of cases all occurred in a small area. Now, new cases are occurring in different countries every day. People around the world are worried that they might catch SARS. In the worst-hit areas, hospitals do not have enough quarantine areas to isolate all the SARS patients. This makes it harder to stop the disease from spreading. People are being urged not to travel abroad. People living in affected areas are wearing face masks when they go out. All students have to wear masks in school. The number of SARS cases is increasing daily. Governments are worried that it is just a matter of time before the outbreak becomes a global crisis.

What is SARS?

Severe acute respiratory syndrome (SARS) was the first new disease to appear in the 21st century. Symptoms usually appear within two to ten days of infection. Patients have a high fever, together with aches and discomfort and a dry cough that makes breathing difficult. SARS is caused by a coronavirus (so called because, when looked at under a microscope, it has the appearance of a crown, or corona) called SARS-CoV. This is the type of virus that causes the common cold and pneumonia. Research in China suggested that the virus originated in horseshoe bats and spread to humans via wild civet cats. Neither the bats nor the cats showed any signs of the illness.

The first outbreak

In November 2002, a patient in Guangdong Province in China was diagnosed with an unusual type of lung infection. The patient, a farmer, died soon afterwards. A doctor became infected too. He then travelled to Hong Kong, carrying the disease with him. From there, the disease spread quickly in Asia, and then to North America, Europe and eventually worldwide.

Why didn't the world react more quickly?

The Chinese authorities delayed reporting the initial outbreak in China to the World Health Organization. For this reason, emergency measures were not taken in the early stages of the outbreak. By the time government health organizations reacted, the disease had spread too far to be easily contained. Some of the ways people tried to restrict the spread of SARS included:

- setting up a worldwide communications network for medical workers to exchange information
- extensive use of quarantine
- screening airline passengers for symptoms of SARS
- using isolation hospitals to treat SARS patients

These students and their teacher in Hong Kong are wearing masks to protect themselves from catching Severe Acute Respiratory Syndrome (SARS). Similar precautions were taken in many schools and workplaces.

Who was affected?

At the beginning of the outbreak, few people understood the risks posed by SARS. Many health workers were infected in the early days, until people realized that SARS patients posed a risk to them too and needed to be isolated. Worldwide, more than 8,000 people became ill with SARS in 2003. Of these, 813 died. The illness was much more severe in people over 65 than in younger age groups.

SARS CASES AND DEATHS IN 2003

	February	March	April	May	June	July
cases	167	1,455	4,041	2,697	87	0
deaths	4	54	314	392	47	2

How does SARS spread?

SARS spreads from person to person via body fluids. It is usually transmitted by droplets of liquid that fly into the air when a person coughs or sneezes. SARS can also be passed on by sexual contact. The virus is contagious at any stage of the infection. This means that people can infect others even before they show any symptoms of the illness themselves. Patients are still considered to be infectious for ten days after the end of the fever.

How is SARS treated?

There is no effective drug treatment for SARS. In many cases all medical staff can do is make patients more comfortable and try to ease their symptoms. Extra oxygen can help patients breathe. Research suggests that some of the worst of the symptoms are caused by the body's immune system over-reacting to the virus. Future treatments may involve drugs that limit the immune response.

Scientists have developed vaccines that are effective against the virus strain responsible for the 2003 SARS outbreak. The vaccines could be used to protect medical workers and others deemed to be at

A medical expert performs tests on the Severe Acute Respiratory Syndrome (SARS) virus at a laboratory in China.

high risk in the event of another SARS outbreak. However, the vaccines may offer only limited, if any, protection against new strains of the SARS virus.

Eradication of SARS

In May 2005, the World Health Organization declared that SARS was officially eradicated. There had been no reports of new cases for more than a year. Now it is believed that the SARS virus exists only in secure laboratories. The disease should never reappear. However, it's possible that SARS could arise again. This could either happen naturally as it did before or someone could let the virus out of the laboratory, by accident or on purpose.

DEBATE

You are in charge
The SARS outbreak has not yet reached your country. As head of the government, you want to keep your country SARS-free. Do you:

- ban all travel into and out of the country, even though that could be disastrous for trade and could affect supplies of food and other essentials?
- ban travel only to and from areas known to have SARS cases, although the disease may have already spread to new areas?
- isolate people arriving in the country for a quarantine period, then allow them in, although this will stretch medical services to the limit?
- screen airline passengers arriving in the country for symptoms of SARS, although you know that no symptoms appear in the early stages of infection?

Which of these do you think would be the best course of action?

CHAPTER 5

Antibiotic-Resistant Infections

It is 2025. Illnesses that had until recently been controllable and posed little risk to human life have become deadly killers. Even a simple cut can lead to a life-threatening infection. This is because antibiotic drugs, once used to treat numerous illnesses and infections, no longer work. Infected patients are nursed in isolation to prevent the infection spreading. Many people are reluctant to go to hospital in case they catch something deadly. Any one of these infections could develop into an epidemic, against which there would be no effective medicine. Scientists are in a race against time to develop new antibiotics. When they do, though, the bacteria rapidly develop resistance to them, and so yet more antibiotics are needed.

What are antibiotic-resistant infections?

Most people have taken antibiotics at some point. These are drugs used to treat many bacterial infections. Some kill the bacteria. Others prevent them from reproducing.

The first antibiotic available for use in patients was penicillin. It was introduced in the late 1940s. Doctors were delighted that at last they had an effective treatment for often-deadly bacterial infections. Before long, however, doctors began to notice that some bacteria were resistant to penicillin.

As more antibiotics were developed during the 1950s and 1960s, their use increased rapidly. So too did the appearance of resistant strains of bacteria. For example, methicillin was introduced in 1960 to treat Staphylococcus aureus (MRSA) infections. The first strains of methicillin-resistant Staphylococcus aureus (MRSA) were reported within a few months.

The green dots in this micrograph are antibiotic-resistant Staphylococcus aureus cells. They are shown on the surface of the small intestine.

Resistant strains of other bacteria have also emerged. Clostridium difficile (C. diff), which causes severe diarrhoea, poses a special problem. Its spores can remain viable (active) for a long time, and until recently there was no known way of killing them. A wide range of bacteria, including Escherichia coli (E. Coli), which causes food poisoning, are also developing resistance to antibiotics.

For many years, scientists have warned of the dangers of over-using antibiotics. However, this advice has largely been ignored. As antibiotic use has continued, increasing numbers of resistant bacterial strains have emerged.

People get antibiotic-resistant infections in one of two ways:

- by catching an already existing antibiotic-resistant strain of bacteria
- by developing a bacterial infection that changes in the body to become resistant to the antibiotic that is being used to treat it.

MRSA CASES IN US HOSPITALS

This graph shows the dramatic increase in the number of MRSA cases in US hospitals between 1993 and 2005. There were fewer than 2,000 cases in 1993, compared to nearly 400,000 cases in 2005.

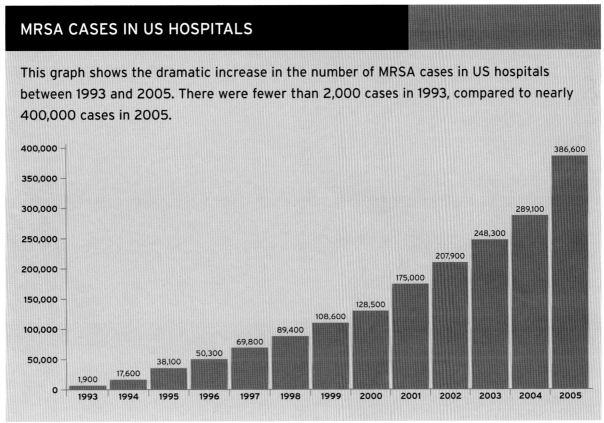

Source: AHRQ, Center for Delivery, Organization, and Markets, Healthcare Cost and Utilization Project, Nationwide Inpatient Sample, 1993-2005

Preventing infections

Hospitals are attempting to reduce the number of antibiotic-resistant infections by improving hygiene. Many are also testing all patients admitted to the hospital. Those with infections are isolated to prevent the infection from spreading.

How can bacteria be antibiotic-resistant?

Like all living organisms, bacteria must evolve and adapt to survive. They can develop resistance to antibiotics by interfering with the ways in which the antibiotics work. For example, penicillin kills bacteria by attaching itself to the bacterial cell wall. It destroys part of the wall and the bacterium dies. Bacteria can become resistant to this action in one of two ways:

- by altering their walls so that the penicillin cannot attach itself to them
- by producing chemicals to dismantle the penicillin molecules

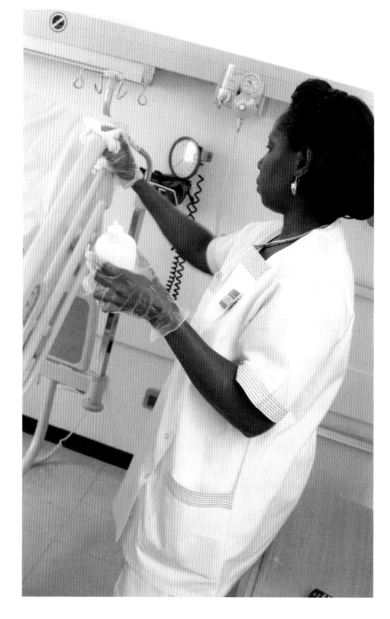

Thorough cleaning and disinfecting of hospital beds and equipment is essential to reduce the spread of infection from patient to patient.

These changes occur in the genetic information of the bacterium, so the changes are maintained in all the new bacteria that develop during the infection.

Antibiotic-resistant tuberculosis

Tuberculosis (TB) is a disease found in most countries of the world. In developing countries, it affects the lungs as well as other organs. In developed countries it is generally confined to the lungs. TB is responsible for nearly two million deaths every year. It is caused by a bacterium called Mycobacterium tuberculosis. It is spread when an infected person coughs or sneezes.

Since the introduction of antibiotics, it has been possible to treat TB effectively. However, in recent years doctors have found some strains of the bacterium that are resistant to antibiotics. Some are resistant to two or more of the antibiotics that would normally be doctors' first choice for treating TB. These strains are known as multi-drug resistant TB, or MDR TB. Patients with MDR TB have to be treated with other drugs that are more expensive and have worse side effects. In 2006, WHO estimated there were about 425,000 cases of MDR TB globally each year. Even worse, strains of TB have appeared that are resistant to all the first-choice drugs and more than six of the second-choice drugs. They are known as extreme drug resistant strains (XDR TB) and are virtually untreatable.

Teams of scientists are investigating the resistant TB strains. They are trying to find out how the bacterium becomes resistant to different drugs, They hope that will help them develop new drugs that the bacterium won't be able to resist.

Out of the hospitals

Initially, antibiotic-resistant infections affected only hospital patients. The immune systems of people who were already sick or weak could not overcome the infections. Recently, though, some strains have been found in healthy people who did not contract them in hospitals. Cases of previously healthy people infected with resistant strains of MRSA have been reported in both North America and Europe. The possibility that such infections could reach epidemic levels is a cause for serious concern, as we would have no effective means of treating them.

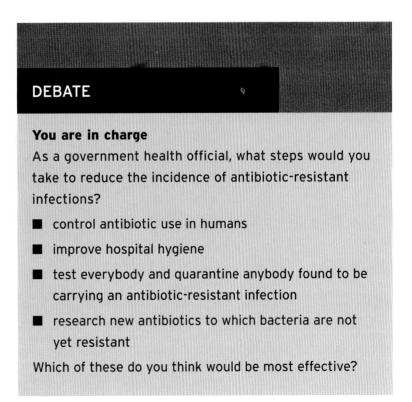

DEBATE

You are in charge
As a government health official, what steps would you take to reduce the incidence of antibiotic-resistant infections?

■ control antibiotic use in humans

■ improve hospital hygiene

■ test everybody and quarantine anybody found to be carrying an antibiotic-resistant infection

■ research new antibiotics to which bacteria are not yet resistant

Which of these do you think would be most effective?

CHAPTER 6

Viral Haemorrhagic Fevers

It is 2025. A fierce viral epidemic is raging throughout large areas of Africa and the Middle East. Many people are sick and the death toll is rising by the day. Authorities try to limit the spread of the infection by clearing rubbish tips and other rat-infested places. Grain is being transferred to rat-proof containers. Governments and aid agencies are telling people not to dispose of waste close to their homes. They are also being encouraged to maintain high standards of hygiene, but this can be difficult in areas where sanitation is poor.

What are viral haemorrhagic fevers?

There are many different viral haemorrhagic fevers (VHFs), including Ebola fever, Marburg fever, Lassa fever and Rift Valley fever. Although each disease is caused by a different virus, there are some similarities between them. They usually affect many organs of the body at the same time and often cause internal bleeding. Symptoms include fever, tiredness, dizziness, aching muscles, weakness and exhaustion. Although some only cause mild illnesses, others are usually fatal. In some cases, antiviral drugs can help, but in many cases there is no effective treatment for these viruses.

Where do VHFs occur?

VHFs generally occur in tropical countries. Each virus occurs within a limited geographic area. This is because they are dependent on an animal or insect host and can only survive in areas where their host species lives. Humans are not the natural host for any of these

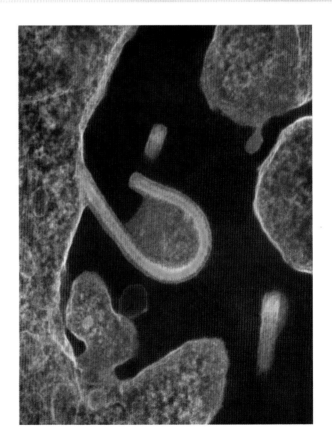

This micrograph shows the release of an Ebola virus (blue and green) from a host cell (green/pink). By taking part of the host cell with it, the virus is able to evade the host's immune system.

viruses. Humans become infected only after coming into contact with infected host animals or insects. Once a human is infected, though, he or she can pass the infection on to other humans.

People occasionally become infected by a host that is far from its native habitat. For example, in 1967, laboratory workers in Marburg, Germany, became infected by monkeys imported from Uganda, which were infected with a virus from that country. The virus came to be called Marburg virus. Also, a person who becomes infected in one place may travel elsewhere and infect other people in other places. With the expansion of international travel, outbreaks of these diseases are appearing in places where they have never been seen before.

How do people become infected?

The means of infection depends to a large extent on the type of animal or insect host. For example, viruses carried by rats and other rodents are usually transmitted when humans come into contact with waste from infected animals. Viruses carried by insects are usually transmitted when an infected insect bites a human. This table shows some examples of VHFs, their hosts and the ways they are transmitted to humans.

SOME VIRAL HAEMORRHAGIC FEVERS

Infection	Host	Means of transmission
Ebola virus	unknown; research suggests a bat species	via body fluids such as blood, faeces and saliva of infected non-human primates (e.g. chimpanzee)
Marburg virus	unknown	uncertain, but possibly via infected non-human primates (e.g. apes and monkeys)
Lassa fever	multimammate rat	contact with infected rats or their waste
Dengue fever	mosquito	mosquito bite
Crimean-Congo fever	tick	tick infects livestock such as cattle, sheep and goats. Humans are then infected via contact with blood or other infected tissues from livestock, or directly by a tick bite.
Rift Valley fever	blood-sucking sandflies	sandfly bite

Preventing viral haemorrhagic infections

Vaccines are available that offer protection against yellow fever and Argentine haemorrhagic fever. However, as yet, no effective vaccines have been developed against the other VHFs. Currently, the only way to prevent infection is to avoid contact with the host species.

For diseases that are spread by rodents, the best ways to avoid infection are to control rodent populations, to discourage rodents from entering or living in homes and workplaces and to encourage the safe clean-up of rodent nests and droppings. Diseases that are spread by insects, such as mosquitoes, may be prevented by using insecticide, insect repellent, clothing to cover the body so the skin is not exposed, mosquito nets and window screens. Diseases that are spread by contact with non-human primates are best prevented by avoiding contact with infected primates.

Researchers in Ivory Coast, Africa, collect the skull of a colobus monkey for testing. They are part of a programme sponsored by the WHO to find the source of the ebola virus. Colobus monkeys are one suspected host. Others include bats and rodents.

When infection occurs

If a person becomes infected with a viral haemorrhagic fever, the local community usually takes steps to prevent the disease from spreading to others. This is best achieved by avoiding close physical contact with the patient and wearing appropriate protective clothing. People caring for the patient need to attend to hygiene and disinfect or safely dispose of medical equipment after use.

Monitoring outbreaks and vectors

Countries report outbreaks of VHFs to the World Health Organization (WHO), which analyses the information. The organization then tries to predict where new outbreaks are likely to occur. This helps governments take precautions to limit the spread of diseases. The WHO analyses a wide variety of data, including environmental factors. For example, if the food supply of rats is particularly abundant in one area, the animal is more likely to thrive, placing people in that area at greater risk of diseases carried by rats.

Into the future

Scientists studying viral haemorrhagic fevers have several aims. Some are working on ways to prevent the spread of infections, such as improved insect control. Others hope to develop effective treatments or vaccines. Other scientists are attempting to improve methods of diagnosis. They are studying how the diseases are transmitted and how they affect the body (a study known as pathogenesis). This will help them to identify these diseases in future.

Scientists studying these viruses risk becoming infected themselves. Therefore, laboratory procedures are designed to make sure the virus does not escape from the containers in which it is kept. Not all laboratories have such a secure environment. However, researchers have found a way to alter the Ebola virus so that it cannot multiply, allowing them to study it in safety. Scientists hope to develop similar techniques for other viruses. Diagnosis and treatments are likely to improve as our knowledge of these diseases increases.

DEBATE

You are in charge

As health minister for a country where haemorrhagic fevers are endemic (cases occur regularly among the population), do you spend your money on

- vector control?
- vaccine development?
- improved medication?
- improved sanitation and hygiene?

Which of these methods do you think would be most effective in controlling the outbreaks of these fevers and why?

Malaria

It is 2025. Millions of people in Africa, India, and the Middle East have malaria. Supplies of medication are running dangerously low. Medical workers are swamped by new cases every day. Newspapers, billboards, radio, television and the Internet spread anti-malaria advice to as many people as possible. As summer approaches, temperatures in Mediterranean countries are rising and cases of malaria are being reported in southern Europe. People are cancelling holidays to areas where malaria is rife and the Mediterranean tourist trade is also being affected. Scientific efforts are directed towards tracking the mosquito population in an attempt to predict where the next outbreak will occur.

What is malaria?

Malaria is a disease that usually occurs in warm countries, especially Africa and Asia. In some places, the number of cases stays much the same all year round. In other areas, the number of cases follows a seasonal pattern, with most cases appearing during the rainy season. More than 500 million people become seriously ill with malaria each year. More than one million die. Children and pregnant women are at greater risk than other groups. According to the World Health Organization, a child dies from malaria every 30 seconds. Malaria symptoms, which include fever, headache, chills and vomiting, usually appear 10 to 15 days after infection.

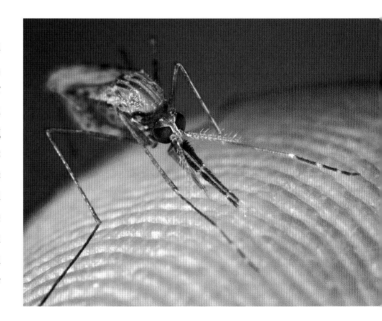

Female Anopheles gambiae mosquitoes like this one, which has been photographed on a human finger, transmit malaria.

What causes malaria?

Malaria is caused by a parasite called *Plasmodium*. There are four species of this parasite that can infect humans, one of which, *Plasmodium falciparum*, causes a far more serious illness than the others. This species is responsible for most malarial deaths.

How does malaria spread?

The Plasmodium parasite infects people through an insect vector: the mosquito. It does not spread directly from human to human. When an infected mosquito bites a human, the mosquito transfers Plasmodium cells into the person's blood. The Plasmodium cells are carried in the blood to the liver, where they reproduce rapidly. The new Plasmodium cells escape back into the bloodstream and enter the red blood cells. The infected red blood cells burst, releasing Plasmodium cells, which in turn infect more red blood cells. Red blood cells' normal function is to carry oxygen around the body. However, the infection prevents them from doing this, so the victim becomes short of oxygen. If another mosquito bites the infected person, it sucks up blood that contains Plasmodium cells. If the mosquito then bites somebody else, it will transfer the infection to them. As this cycle continues, more and more people become infected.

The malarial cycle involves Plasmodium parasites, mosquitoes and humans. This diagram shows how the three are linked, and how the disease is spread.

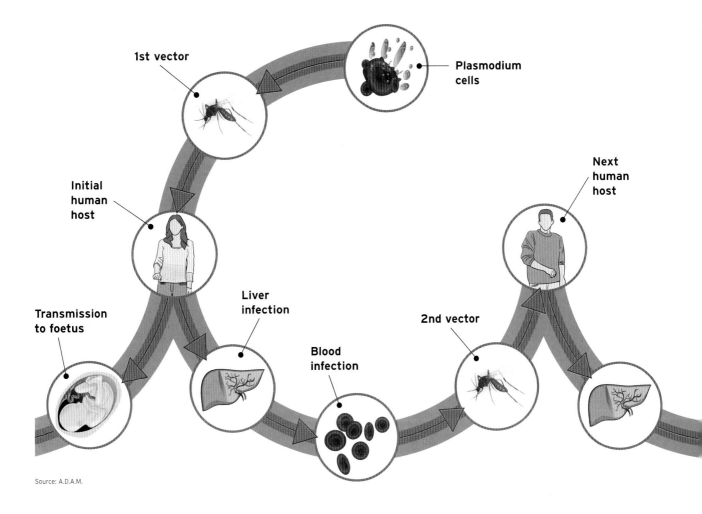

1st vector

Plasmodium cells

Initial human host

Next human host

Transmission to foetus

Liver infection

Blood infection

2nd vector

Source: A.D.A.M.

Treating malaria

Malaria isn't a serious illness if it's diagnosed and treated early. A traditional remedy for malaria is a drug called quinine. Modern medicines, based on a chemical called artemisinin, can kill Plasmodium cells. However, widespread use of these medicines has created strains of drug-resistant Plasmodium. Despite intensive research, there are as yet no effective alternatives to artemisinin medicines for the treatment of malaria.

Avoiding malaria

Individuals can reduce their risk of catching malaria by taking a few simple precautions. These include taking anti-malarial drugs, keeping skin covered, using an insect repellent and sleeping underneath an insecticide-treated mosquito net. Travellers to malaria-prone regions are usually able to follow these guidelines. However, people who live in such countries often lack the resources to protect themselves.

A young volunteer helps a health worker demonstrate the correct way to use a mosquito net in Antsokia Woreda, Ethiopia. The nets are being distributed as part of a campaign against malaria, Ethiopia's most deadly disease.

An effective anti-malaria vaccine is not yet available. However, scientists hope that one will soon be developed. One team has found a way of interfering with the reproduction of Plasmodium cells and they hope that this has the potential to lead to an effective vaccine.

Controlling malaria outbreaks

Most efforts to control malaria involve reducing the mosquito population. Without mosquitoes, the Plasmodium parasites cannot infect humans. The insecticides DDT and pyrethrum are both effective against the mosquitoes. However, insecticide-resistant mosquito strains are developing. Research is continuing into other ways to control the mosquito population. One method involves introducing a natural predator such as the mosquitofish, which eats the mosquitoes.

Malaria and sickle cell anaemia

Sickle cell anaemia is a blood disorder. It occurs in the same parts of the world as malaria. People with sickle cell anaemia have distorted red blood cells that cannot carry oxygen efficiently. The condition is inherited, but only people who inherit a sickle cell gene from each parent develop full sickle cell anaemia. People who inherit a single sickle cell gene from just one parent will have a milder condition called sickle cell trait. Scientists have found that, although sickle cell anaemia can cause serious illness, there is some benefit in having sickle cell trait, as it offers some protection against malaria. This is because the Plasmodium cells cannot survive in the distorted red blood cells. Studies of people with sickle cell trait have given scientists new insights into how the immune system can fight malaria.

DEBATE

You are in charge
You run a tourism company in a country where malaria is endemic. What is your advice to people visiting your country?
- take anti-malarial medication before, during and after your trip
- use mosquito nets at night
- use insect repellent
- don't come!

Which of these precautions do you think would best protect tourists against malaria, and bring in more business?

Meningitis

It is 2025. A few weeks ago, a case of meningitis was reported in a young child, who died in hospital. Despite rapid vaccination of all the boy's close contacts, within days children from the same school showed symptoms of the infection. More lives were lost. The vaccination programme widened but it appears to have been too late. More cases are appearing. Doctors fear a major epidemic is about to grip the country. Although some cases have been seen in adults, most victims have been young children. Many parents are keeping their children at home until the crisis is over. Schools and nurseries in badly hit areas are closing to reduce the risk of children passing the infection on to others. People everywhere hope the worst is over, but fear there may be many more deaths.

What is meningitis?

Meningitis is an infection of the meninges, the lining of the brain and spinal cord. There are two types: viral meningitis and bacterial meningitis. Viral meningitis is rarely serious, causing flu-like symptoms from which most people recover quickly. Bacterial meningitis is much more serious. It can cause brain damage or even death if not treated quickly. Several different bacteria can cause meningitis, but *Neisseria meningitidis* (meningococcus) is the most important because it is most likely to pass from person to person.

What are the symptoms of meningitis?

Meningococcal meningitis can cause symptoms within just a few hours of entering the body. The first sign is often a rash of small purple-red spots, which spread rapidly. Unlike most rashes, a meningitis rash does not fade when it is pressed. Babies and young children often become either stiff or very floppy. They breathe rapidly and have a high fever. Older children and adults often suffer from a stiff neck, severe headache, sensitivity to light, fever and other symptoms such as muscle cramps.

If meningitis is suspected, the patient is usually taken immediately to hospital. The doctor removes a small amount of fluid from the patient's spine, a procedure known as a lumbar puncture. Tests on the fluid will show whether the meningococcus bacteria is present.

What treatments are available?

Doctors usually give patients antibiotics as soon as possible. However, antibiotics cannot be given before the lumbar sample is taken. Killing the bacteria could give a negative diagnosis. If a small number of live bacteria survive undetected, they will multiply and the infection will worsen. To speed the treatment, medical staff deliver antibiotics directly into the bloodstream. Close monitoring of the patient's condition is essential to check that no complications develop.

What are the long-term effects?

Meningococcal meningitis can be fatal. People who recover often suffer long-term effects, such as damage to eyesight and hearing.

A mother tests her daughter for meningitis by pressing a clear glass against her skin. A common symptom of meningitis is a blotchy skin rash, which does not fade under pressure. If the rash does not fade, medical help should be sought immediately.

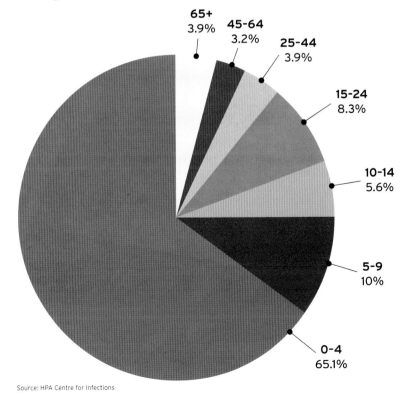

65+
3.9%

45-64
3.2%

25-44
3.9%

15-24
8.3%

10-14
5.6%

5-9
10%

0-4
65.1%

Source: HPA Centre for Infections

This pie chart shows the percentage of meningitis cases in different age groups in one year in England and Wales. Nearly two-thirds of the cases were in children under five years old.

39

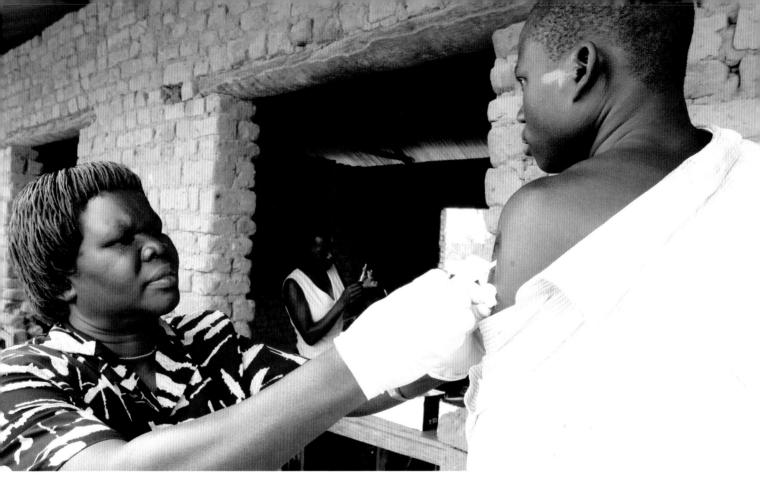

How does meningitis spread?

The meningococcal bacteria pass from person to person through droplets expelled by coughing or sneezing. Being close to an infected person and sharing eating and drinking utensils increases the chance of infection. If someone becomes infected, the people who live with the victim are most at risk.

How can the spread of meningitis be prevented or limited?

Several actions can help reduce the spread of meningitis. These include:

- **Routine vaccination** In some countries, an entire population is vaccinated. Saudi Arabia, for example, offers routine vaccination for everyone. In Sudan and some other countries, schoolchildren are vaccinated.
- **Preventive vaccination** This can be used for people travelling to an area where there is an outbreak of meningitis.
- **Protection of close contacts** When a case of meningitis is diagnosed, people who have been in close contact with the patient need to be protected by a vaccine and antibiotics.

A health worker injects a man with a meningitis vaccine in Uganda. In a massive campaign in 2007, more than 300,000 people in one district were vaccinated in just three weeks.

Where and when does meningitis occur?

Meningococcal meningitis outbreaks occur worldwide, in small clusters. Most countries have reported outbreaks at some time. However, outbreaks are particularly common in poor, overcrowded areas in developing countries, especially in the 'meningitis belt' of Africa that stretches from Senegal, The Gambia and Guinea in the west to Sudan and Ethiopia in the east.

Meningitis outbreaks seem to be affected by the seasons. In temperate regions, such as Europe and the United States, most cases occur during winter and spring. In Africa and Asia, they are most likely to occur during the dry season between December and June.

Controlling an epidemic

Countries prone to meningitis constantly monitor the situation to pinpoint outbreaks quickly. This enables them to give antibiotics as soon as possible. The World Health Organization recommends mass vaccination in the area where an epidemic begins and in areas close by. Experts estimate that if mass vaccination is carried out promptly, 70 per cent of cases will be avoided.

DEBATE

You are in charge
There have been a few isolated cases of meningitis in your country. As head of public information for the government, how would you raise public awareness of the signs of meningitis and give advice about what to do if a case is suspected?

- distribute posters and leaflets in hospitals, health centres, libraries and other public places
- broadcast information on television and radio
- print articles in newspapers and magazines
- send letters to every household
- put information on the Internet

Which do you think would be most effective and why?

CHAPTER 9

Gone But Not Forgotten

It is 2025. A polio epidemic is sweeping through America, leaving people paralysed or, in the most serious cases, dead. The first reported case involved a girl who came to study in the United States from India, where polio is still widespread. A mass vaccination programme had made polio rare in the United States. After decades without polio, many Americans thought their children no longer needed the vaccine. As a result, the virus is now spreading rapidly among unvaccinated children. Health officials have launched a mass vaccination campaign. They are also alerting doctors, many of whom had never seen a case of polio before. More and more people are being diagnosed every day. Some countries are considering quarantine restrictions on people travelling from America, to prevent the epidemic spreading even further.

How could this happen?

Polio, or poliomyelitis, is a viral infection that attacks the nerves and the brain. Until the middle of the 20th century, polio was common in the United States. During the 1950s, vaccines were developed. Mass vaccination led to a rapid decrease in the number of cases of polio. By the 1970s, Americans began to view polio as a disease of the past. Like many contagious diseases, however, polio is just a plane ride away. Mass vaccination programmes have eradicated diseases from some countries. But unless everyone is vaccinated, people are still at risk. Some diseases have been wiped out worldwide. Today, the viruses that caused them exist only in laboratories. Yet even these pose a threat.

Out of the lab

The micro-organisms that cause some deadly diseases still exist in laboratories around the world. Some are kept for legitimate research purposes. For example, because deadly bubonic plague (which once wiped out a quarter of Europe's population) still occurs naturally in some parts of the world, research into new treatments and vaccines is necessary. Therefore, a laboratory may need to use a sample of the micro-organism that causes plague. Also, such biological materials may be needed to research treatments for future biological weapons. These biological materials could find their way into the general population either by accident or by intention as a biological weapon.

A scientist conducts research in a laboratory with a very high level of biosecurity. He is wearing a protective suit with helmet, and his face mask is supplied with air via overhead lines that plug into the suit.

MINIMIZING LABORATORY RISKS

There is always a small chance that dangerous, infectious biological material might get out of a laboratory and cause an epidemic or pandemic. To minimize this risk, laboratories need to maintain high standards of safety and security. Laboratories follow safety guidelines to minimize the risk of dangerous material escaping. Official inspections ensure that people take safety precautions. These include having a filtered ventilation system, working in biological safety cabinets and wearing protective clothing. Tight laboratory security is maintained to reduce the possibility of any dangerous material being stolen.

Eradicating infectious diseases

In an ideal world, infectious diseases would not exist. This may not be achievable, but there are worldwide programmes in place to eradicate individual diseases. The World Health Organization (WHO) began a programme to eradicate smallpox in 1967. The last case of smallpox was reported in 1977. The WHO declared the disease officially eradicated in 1980. Diseases spread in many different ways. That means scientists need to use different approaches to eradicate them. For some diseases, developing a vaccine is the best solution. Other diseases can be controlled and eliminated by improving sanitation and hygiene.

SOME INFECTIOUS DISEASES AND THEIR CHANCES OF ERADICATION

Disease	Possible obstacles	Eradicable?
Polio	technically possible; needs greater national/international commitment	yes
Guinea worm disease	lack of awareness; inadequate funding to make water supplies safe	yes
Pork tapeworm	need better diagnostic tests for humans and pigs	potentially
Hepatitis B	some people are carriers; cannot prevent infection of baby before birth; infant vaccination needed	not at present, but could be reduced over time
Rabies	vaccines effective on pets but can't vaccinate all wild animals	no, but could be eliminated in towns and cities

Success story

Polio is an example of significant success in the battle against an infectious disease. It is now very rare for a case of polio to arise in the developed world. However, the disease is still endemic in Nigeria, Afghanistan, India and Pakistan. In 1988, the Global Polio Eradication Initiative was launched. Children around the world were vaccinated. As a result, the incidence of polio has decreased from 350,000 cases per year in 1988 to just 1,313 in 2007. Scientists hope that further vaccination programmes will eradicate the disease completely.

Vigilance is necessary, though. Somalia, declared polio-free in 2002, became re-infected from Nigeria in 2005. However, the last case was reported in March 2007 and in March 2008 the country was again declared polio-free.

Scientists and health experts are convinced that some other deadly infectious diseases could be eradicated. However, international commitment and co-operation, together with adequate funding, are essential if this is to be achieved.

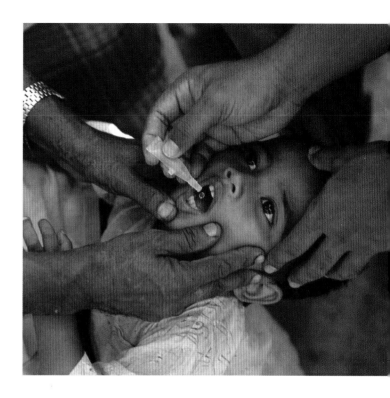

Just two drops of polio vaccine will protect this Bangladeshi boy from a virus that once crippled millions of children. Global efforts have almost eradicated polio.

DEBATE

You are in charge

You run the government's vaccination programme. Many people think they do not need vaccines for diseases that are no longer a problem in your country. Others worry about the safety of vaccines. You know how easily diseases spread from one country to the next and you know that vaccines are safe and effective ways to prevent that. How do you convince people to get vaccinated?

■ You develop a public awareness campaign about vaccine safety and the importance of vaccinations.

■ You make sure every doctor has information about vaccine safety to hand out to patients.

■ You make vaccines compulsory for every child before they are allowed to attend school.

Which of these options do you think would be the most effective way of persuading people to get vaccinated?

Glossary

abstinence Refraining from doing something.

antibiotic A medicine used to treat bacterial infections.

antibody A protein produced by white blood cells in response to the presence of a bacterium or virus.

antiviral A medicine used to treat viral infections.

bacteria A type of micro-organism that can reproduce independently.

caesarean section A surgical procedure that can be used to deliver a child.

cell One of the tiny units of which all living things are made.

contagious Transmitted from one person to another by direct contact.

cull Kill part of an animal population, for example to prevent an epidemic.

diagnose Identify an illness or disorder.

domesticated Cultivated, raised or bred for human requirements.

endemic Occurring naturally in a particular place.

epidemic An outbreak of an infectious disease that affects many people.

eradicate Completely destroy, so that it is unable to recur.

fungi A type of micro-organism that reproduces by spores and lives by absorbing nutrients from organic matter.

genetic To do with passing information from one generation to the next.

host An organism that a micro-organism infects.

hygiene Health and cleanliness.

immune system The body's defence against infection and other illnesses.

immunity Resistance to a particular infection.

infectious Describing something that can spread from person to person.

inherited Passed from one generation to the next.

micro-organism An organism that is too small to be seen with the naked eye.

mutate Undergo a genetic change, resulting in a new characteristic.

pandemic An outbreak of an infection affecting many people over a very large area.

parasite An organism that lives on or in another (host) organism in a way that harms or is of no advantage to the host.

primate A member of the order of mammals that includes humans, apes and monkeys.

quarantine Keep away from others to prevent the spread of infection.

refugee Someone who seeks refuge, especially from war or persecution, by going to a foreign country.

sanitation maintenance of public health and hygiene, especially the water supply and sewage systems.

spore The reproductive structure of some micro-organisms.

sterile Free from living bacteria or other micro-organisms.

strain A subgroup of a species of organism.

Sub-Saharan Africa The region of Africa that lies south of the Sahara. It includes the countries of East, central, West and southern Africa.

surveillance Continual observation of something or someone.

symptom An indication of a disease or some other disorder.

transfusion The process of giving a patient blood from another person.

transmission Passing from one person or thing to another.

vaccine A substance used to produce immunity from a particular infection.

vector An organism, such as a mosquito, that transmits disease-causing micro-organisms from infected individuals to other people, or from infected animals to human beings.

veterinary To do with diseases of animals and their treatment.

virus A type of micro-organism that cannot reproduce independently.

World Health Organization (WHO) An agency of the United Nations that coordinates international efforts to fight disease and promote health.

Further Information

Books

At Issue: Pandemics by David M Haugen, Susan Musser (Greenhaven Press, 2007)

Deadly Disasters: The AIDS Epidemic: Disaster & Survival by Jennifer Reed (Enslow Publishers, 2005)

DK Eyewitness: Epidemic by Brian Ward (Dorling Kindersley, 2000)

In the News: Epidemics by Ann Kramer (Franklin Watts, 2006)

In the News: Pandemics: Epidemics in a Shrinking World by Miriam Segall (Rosen Publishing Group, 2007)

Kingfisher Knowledge: Epidemics and Plagues by Denise Grady, Richard Walker (Kingfisher Books, 2006)

Mapping Epidemics: A Historical Atlas of Disease by Brent H Hoff, Carter Smith, Charles H Calisher (Franklin Watts, 2000)

Opposing Viewpoints: Epidemics by Mary E Williams, Bruce Glassman, Bonnie Szumski (Greenhaven Press, 2005)

Websites

library.thinkquest.org/11170/
Site with information about infectious diseases, maps, how epidemics arise, quizzes – and more!

www.archives.gov/exhibits/influenza-epidemic/
Find out about the influenza epidemic of 1918 from original pictures and records.

www.amnh.org/exhibitions/epidemic/section_08/index.html
A good source of information about epidemics and pandemics from the American Natural History Museum.

www.avert.org/
A wealth of information about HIV/AIDS.

Debate Panel answers

Page 7:
If information about diagnosed cases of infectious diseases is collected centrally, it can be analysed regularly. This should allow authorities to spot trends and provide early warning of an epidemic developing. Detailed information about the location, age, sex, ethnic group and recent travel of those infected can all help to build up a more complete picture of what is happening. Each of these would be helpful in monitoring the outbreak of an epidemic.

Page 13:
Education about how to avoid infection should, if people follow the advice, reduce the number of new cases of HIV/AIDS. Available medicines for treating HIV/AIDS are very expensive and active steps to achieve a reduction in their cost would benefit many. An effective vaccine would protect those not yet infected but would be of no benefit to existing sufferers. For a developing country, spending on scientific research would be low-priority, as this would be better done in well-funded laboratories in the developed world; it is probably more important for a developing country to spend money on education and buying drugs to keep people alive.

Page 21:
Key workers include medical staff who would help anyone who became ill. It would therefore be sensible to vaccinate these people first. After that, the most vulnerable would be in greatest need of protection. Most people would think it unfair to vaccinate those who could pay and leave the poor at risk, or to allocate vaccinations on a random 'first come, first served' basis.

Page 25:
Banning all travel into and out of the country could have a disastrous economic effect, as well as disrupting supplies of food and other essentials. Banning travel to and from SARS-affected areas, while at the same time quarantining arrivals from other areas, would greatly reduce the risk of a SARS outbreak in the country. However, this would be very costly and may prove impractical. Screening arrivals may prove to be the only viable option – even if it would not prevent the possibility of a SARS outbreak.

Page 29:
Controlling antibiotic use in humans and animals could help to slow down the development of new antibiotic-resistant strains. Improving hospital hygiene would help to reduce infections. Testing and quarantining patients would help to prevent the infection spreading. Each of these has a part to play in reducing the incidence of antibiotic-resistant infections. Developing new antibiotics would offer treatment against those resistant strains that already exist, but would probably result in the appearance of even more resistant strains.

Page 33:
Without the vector, these micro-organisms cannot infect humans and so vector control can play a big part in helping to reduce these infections. Effective vaccines would help to prevent future infections, while improved medication would reduce the severity of the infection. Although poor communities would generally benefit from improved sanitation and hygiene, this would only help control those infections where lack of sanitation played a part in transmission.

Page 37:
Advising people not to visit your country would be disastrous for your business. It would also affect the economy as a whole and cause unemployment for many people. Travellers could be encouraged to visit, provided they heed the advice about anti-malarial medication, mosquito nets and insect-repellent.

Page 41:
Think about where you, your friends and family would be most likely to access such information. Do you take any notice of posters and leaflets in public places? Do you get information from television and radio or are you more likely to look at current affairs on the Internet? Do you read newspapers regularly? How much do you think it would cost to send letters to every household – and would you read them if you received them? Thinking about where you get your information from can help you decide on effective ways of reaching the population as a whole.

Page 45:
If people understood more about the dangers of some infectious diseases, vaccine safety and the importance of vaccinations, they might be persuaded to get vaccinated. Raising public awareness about these issues could therefore be an effective way of achieving your goal. Providing leaflets for doctors to hand out would be a good way of making sure people had accurate information, but would only reach those people who had visited a doctor. You would still need to find ways of reaching the rest of the population. Making vaccination compulsory for all children would certainly increase the numbers vaccinated, although there is a good chance that some people would object to enforced vaccination.

Index

Page numbers in **bold** refer to illustrations and charts.